Weeds
in my
Garden

2015

Angela LeBlanc

Weeds in my Garden

TATE PUBLISHING
AND ENTERPRISES, LLC

Published by Tate Publishing & Enterprises, LLC
127 E. Trade Center Terrace | Mustang, Oklahoma 73064 USA
1.888.361.9473 | www.tatepublishing.com

Tate Publishing is committed to excellence in the publishing industry. The company reflects the philosophy established by the founders, based on Psalm 68:11,
"The Lord gave the word and great was the company of those who published it."

Book design copyright © 2015 by Tate Publishing, LLC. All rights reserved.
Cover design by Ivan Charlem Igot
Interior design by Gram Telen

Published in the United States of America

ISBN: 978-1-68142-266-4
1. Religion / Christian Life / Inspirational
2. Religion / Christian Life / Spiritual Growth
15.04.29

This garden and this book are dedicated
to
Danielle Wright

Contents

Introduction   9

1   Weeds That Spread   11

2   Weeds with Seeds   19

3   Weeds with Strong Roots   29

4   Weeds That Poison   35

5   Perennial versus Annual   41

6   Spending Time in Your Garden   45

7   The Seasons of Life   53

Afterword   59

Introduction

We are all familiar with the *first* garden, the Garden of Eden. One can only imagine how every plant was perfectly placed in the perfect spot, every tree magnificently formed providing abundant fruit for all of God's creatures, every animal and insect had its place, and every day was promised with perfect weather we rarely experience for any length of time in our world today. Although living in the Garden of Eden was paradise, Adam and Eve somehow stepped outside of the Word of God, thinking they knew more than He and ultimately were shunned from paradise to face the world on their own, making their own choices and dealing with the consequences of their choices. God did not leave them but instead gave them the opportunity to find their way back home to Him through His grace and love.

Now close your eyes and visualize your own garden. Is your garden uniform in style with all flowers and shrubs symmetrical? Or is your garden overgrown with weeds suffocating the flowers you planted in spring? Our life is much like a garden. We have an image of what we want our garden of life to resemble, but in reality our lives are filled with problems, making our lives less perfect than the image we expect it to be.

Consider your life in a larger scale. Think beyond your home and include your community, your job, and everything you come in contact with daily as part of your garden of life. Do you like what you see? Is everything in order? Is everything where it should be? Or, like me, do you have issues to deal with and problems to tackle that hold you back from enjoying your garden of life?

If you do not like where you are in life, and you feel overwhelmed by your troubles, allow this book to offer comfort and help you "weed your garden" from your troubles and help you find everlasting peace in God's love. With God's grace, we have the opportunity to have our own Garden of Eden in a sense—holding on to these powerful facts: first, He will protect us from what harms us; second, He shelters us from outside evil; and third, He will deliver us home to live with Him in His Kingdom forever and ever.

1

Weeds That Spread

Pretend we are in my garden together. As we enter the garden gate and see the numerous flower beds arranged along the weather-aged picket fence, we observe weeds spreading across the ground, hugging the earth closely so as not to be noticed but aggressively conquering the freshly tilled soil with their long tentacle roots. Cypress vine is a great example of this type of weed. The delicate vine has a beautiful red flower similar to the morning glory flower. As the fast-growing vine stretches its lacy foliage in all directions, its tubular stems extend from the main plant like the fingers on a hand. As the cypress vine grows, it twists around any plant within its reach. Initially as the vine twists around the plant, the vine holds the plant stationary, not allowing the plant to grow, and ultimately suffocating it once the vine completely covers every limb of its victim.

In life, problems can act the same way. One bad decision sets in motion numerous other bad decisions and eventually collapsing the world around us. For example, when I was at the peak of my career as a real estate attorney, my income was sufficient to provide me with a comfortable life. But as my income increased, my desires for those "pricier toys" increased. No longer did my Timex watch seem to work as well as it did in law school. Instead, a beautiful Rolex watch, with a sparkling diamond bezel worked and looked better, and of course, I thought I deserved it. Instead of paying cash for this perfect watch at the jewelry store, I paid the balance due with a credit card. I knew I would be able to earn enough to pay for it over the next year. And besides, I wanted it now. This impulsive desire to have this luxury item now and pay for it later became a suffocating weed I let grow in my garden of life. Like the cypress vine that starts from a seed and quickly grows outward and upward in all directions, I started a charging habit that would quickly take root and soon completely overtake my garden of life.

Over the next few years, it got easier and easier for me to borrow and charge on credit. There were several instances where lenders would only need to look at my profit and loss statement and give me whatever I requested with a handshake and a signature. At one particular time, I had five credit cards maxed out, two mortgages on one house, one mortgage on a second home, two large car notes, and three business loans. So what was the problem?

Like those weeds creeping along the ground, the first payments were not a problem. I paid the monthly payments, and everyone was happy. I had my toys, and the lender was making a fortune off the interest I was paying for the advanced credit. But like weeds that start growing and taking precious water from the plant they surround, the payments became a struggle when in 2005 the real estate market bubble collapsed. With the number of real estate closings dwindling now by more than fifty percent, my income drop substantially. Making monthly payments now became an endless struggle.

Soon I found myself sitting at the dining room table, trying to decide which bill had to be paid first, which creditor I could delay, and then which lender would report the late payments to the credit bureau. I had to decide how to live on what little was left after the monthly payments were made. And if this chore was not hard enough, I got to go through the same routine every month without any hope of getting out of debt in the near future.

But like invasive weeds, my financial problems could be controlled once I realized I had a financial problem. As I calculated the amount I owed was far more than my gross income would be over the next three years, I had to come up with a plan to get out of this financial wreck. First, I wrote down every personal and business debt I owed. This task was hard because I soon realized I could not remember what I used the credit card for, and what each balance represented. Also now, I owed an amount that would take ten years to pay back if I continued to make only the minimum payments.

As I prayed for help, God let me know in no uncertain terms, *it was time for me to weed my garden of life.* I drafted my list of debts and assets. With the asset list, I prioritized the assets I needed to keep and decided to eliminate those assets that were strictly for pleasure and not a necessity for my family. Both the debt and asset list had to be shortened in order to overcome these financial struggles.

To get to this point, I had to be totally honest with myself and with God. He could only help me as much as I was willing to help myself. In order to get free of these chains of debt, I prayed for Him to give me guidance in making these very hard decisions. Alone I had created my mess, but with His guidance, I had a means of getting my life back on track.

Conquering the debt list was the first priority. The mortgages on the property had the highest balances of all the debts I owed. Did I have to keep this home? Of course not. Did I want to sell this home? Of course not. But was it worth keeping if the cost could land me into bankruptcy? Of course not. As sad as I was about the decision of selling the family home, I knew I needed to sell it in order to regain financial stability. Not only would the sale of the home reduce the amount of total debt I owed, but also the equity in the home would enable me to reduce other debts, as well.

In Luke 14:28, Jesus said, "For which of you, desiring to build a tower, does not first sit down and count the cost, whether he has enough to complete it?" Many times our needs are replaced with our desires, and the long-term effect of our desires is not properly measured against the costly price paid for those desires. The cost of this home, which I had made huge sacrifices for, now exceeded the reduced income I now was earning due to the unforeseen downturn of the economy.

While realizing I was on a different page in life with the reduced real estate demand causing a reduction in my income, standing still while debt was piling up created a burden that I could not physically or emotionally handle. Through prayer, God instructed me in a dream that selling the home was necessary. Listening to His guidance, I promptly listed the house for sale and the house sold quickly.

The new home we were able to purchase after the sale of this house was worth far less than this house we sold. But as a blessing, the new house payment was one-fourth the amount of the previous house payment, and the debt was reduced by two-thirds of the previous mortgage balances I owed. With the reduced house payment, I was able to pay the credit card balances off quicker than I originally estimated. Every day I thank God for delivering me from the chains of frivolous debt. I still have debt, but because of His guidance, I now live within my means and do not struggle monthly to make ends meet. With less worries, I now find it easier to smile and enjoy my days.

The next step to conquering my debt was to cut up my credit cards to eliminate the temptation to use them in the future. It is important to note when you are in the process of eliminating debt; do not close the credit card accounts with creditors because a closed account may cause your credit score to drop. Keeping a good credit score is very important because with a low score, you pay higher interest rates on borrowed money. After cutting up the cards, I prioritized the balances of my credit cards by paying first the one with lowest balance. As one card was paid off, I increased the payment on the next credit card with the lowest balance, and soon this card's balance would diminish as the first. While this technique sounded easy, the term was not. It took four long years before all credit cards were paid in full. The discipline to manage debt was a constant struggle, but the reward of not having financial chains has been worth the sacrifice.

In Proverbs 22:7, it says, "The rich rules over the poor and the borrower is a slave to the lender." As a lender, you should share your blessings with others, offering them hope when they are in need. As a debtor, you are indebted to someone else. What you borrow is not truly yours until the debt is paid in full.

Think of unnecessary and frivolous debt like sin. The more unnecessary debt we have, the less freedom we have to spend our resources the way we need to for ourselves and our family. We are committing future earnings to someone else. Like a frivolous debt, when we consciously sin, we are jeopardizing our soul's future, establishing a bond with the devil, which may prohibit our soul from entering the gates of heaven. Think long and hard about this question. Is that sin you commit today worth the price of everlasting life?

You need to decide today if your earthly pleasures give you complete happiness. With all of your belongings around you, do you still feel lonely? Like the debtor who sits at the dining table looking through the stack of bills, deciding which ones to pay first, sins can stack up against us, making our souls feel lost and not knowing where to turn for help. But like debt consolidation, you too can consolidate your sins into complete forgiveness from God. Jesus died on the cross so that we would be forgiven for all of our sins.

Accepting Jesus Christ as our Savior will give us the spiritual freedom from the shackles of despair, loneliness, and self-destruction. Ask God today to forgive you for your sins. "If we confess our sins, he is faithful and just to forgive us (our) sins and to cleanse us from all unrighteousness" (John 1:9). As we live our lives for God instead of for ourselves, we will be blessed by God's grace, and we will start to realize His love is all we need for complete happiness.

I believe God gives us children so we can experience the parent-child relationship and understand our relationship with Him is of the same type. He wants the best for all of His children. He makes certain we are protected by His grace and are sheltered from the evil that looms over our souls.

2

Weeds with Seeds

Have you ever had a thistle weed grow in your garden? The plant surrounds itself with long needles on every leaf of its green foliage. It is crowned with a delicate white bloom, which contains hundreds of tiny feather-covered seeds just waiting for a big gust of wind to come and spread the seeds over the surrounding ground. One week later after the seeds have been scattered over the premises, there are hundreds of little thistle plants coming up all over the yard. If you had taken the time to pull up the original thistle weed before it bloomed, then you would not have the work of pulling the other hundred weeds that came up from its seeds. Last year, I made it my personal challenge to mow down every thistle weed as it came up in my field. Even though it was too early to mow, my neighbors laughed as they watched me purposefully mow zigzag lines in the field over each tender thistle that proudly gleamed green in the winter brown grass. Because I went through this exerted effort last spring, I did not have any thistle weeds come up this year.

Think how problems are like thistle weeds. Once a problem comes up, and if it is not dealt with immediately, numerous other problems soon develop all stemming from the original problem. Stress is a great example of a problem that needs to be dealt with immediately because long-term stress can kill you.

For years, I did not handle stress well. I believed it was my responsibility to control everything and everybody to make their lives easier, which only made me a person whom few people wanted to be around. I think the clinical term for this type of personality is control freak. The more I took control, the more stress I bottled up to prohibit anyone from seeing the load I carried was heavy and far more than I could manage.

Several years after undergoing a tremendous stressful pattern of working twelve hours a day and then running home and being super mom and wife to my family, my health began to fail. As people would say, "You need to take care of yourself," I would quickly answer back, "I do not have time." As I look back on what I said then, I realize now this was a very stupid response. Not paying attention to my health, my body decided to give me a visual of what was going on inside of me. First, my lips and tongue started swelling at the most inopportune moment. Now when I say *swelling*, I mean it was to the point where my face was completely disfigured like a cartoon character out of a *SpongeBob* episode. Within a five-minute span, I would go looking from normal to looking like a complete monster with eyes completely shut and lips so swollen I could not drink for fear of water running down my chin. Talk about scaring people; I would be conducting a real estate closing, and—*boom*—my face would start swelling. The clients would look at me with huge eyes, wondering if I was about to explode. I would laugh and tell them not to worry, my face will go back to normal in about an hour. Inside I was not laughing because the unpredictability of these scary episodes made my life hell. After seeing several doctors who had no idea what was wrong, I decided this weird occurrence was just something I would just have to live with.

Then the next symptoms set in. First, my heart would race to the point where I felt as if I was physically coming out of my skin. Second, I would get so hot I would come close to passing out. Of course everyone said it was caused from hormone disorder, but again, after several more blood tests and doctor opinions, there was no answer for my progressive illness.

The last symptom made me stop and realize what I had was serious. I started seeing four of everything. My eyes were bulging out of my head. Not being able to see is a problem for someone who drafts legal documents all day. I realized I needed to see what my problem was and how to get it fixed. I made an appointment with an ENT specialist, who suggested I see a particular endocrinologist about my unusual symptoms. As I explained to the ENT that I had tried to get in to see this specialist, but he was no longer taking new patients, he smiled and said, "Let me call him." I had an appointment the very next day with this endocrinologist.

I believe God put this ENT in my path that day to get me the help I needed to cure my illness. When the endocrinologist reviewed my chart, he explained I had Graves' disease which is brought on by long-term stress. He suggested we take an aggressive approach to reaching a cure. The very next day I had a radiation treatment, which killed my thyroid over a short period of time. After the thyroid was killed, I started taking the prescribed synthetic thyroid medicine, and my symptoms soon diminished.

But the root of the problem—stress—had to be dealt with internally. I learned the illness was now under control, but if I continued to let the stress build as before, my body would continue to suffer in other ways. I have learned to manage my stress by putting my problems in God's hands and have learned to patiently wait for things to work themselves out. I am happy to report my vision has corrected itself, my eyes are back in the sockets where they belong and are no longer bulging out, and I have not suffered from a swelling spell since.

The point I am trying to make is not that I got sick and overcame the illness, but—like the thistle that is left to bloom—because I did not handle my problem of stress early on, I developed a serious medical condition that could have killed me. All of this could have been avoided if I had never become stressed in the first place or dealt with the stress early on. Well today, I know that answer. As I practice my faith daily, I know every day God still sits on the throne. He has given me this day to live. I cannot change what happened yesterday, and I have no guarantee tomorrow will come. God has promised this day, and I will make the most of it. Faith in God gives me peace. There is no need to stress over things we cannot change. There is no need to stress over things that have already occurred. What I try to do every day is be the best person I can be, deal with the issues of the day, and only worry about what I can do and not what others do or fail to do.

I save time for myself each and every day to thank God for the blessings I have received and those that will be coming in my future. When I find myself beginning to feel stressed, I simply say out loud, "God you are in charge. Lead me through this valley." If you are under an enormous amount of stress today, maybe it is time to turn those problems over to God and let Him be in control. He knows our past, our present, and our future. Walking the path He has prepared for us is the only way we can walk this earth with little or no stress. "For nothing is impossible with God" (Luke 1:37). Step up and allow God to remove the chains of stress you are feeling today by accepting His arms of strength and continuous support.

Look at your garden of life. Are there any weeds you need to deal with, which, if not pulled today, may bring you more heartache in the future? The old saying, "Don't put off tomorrow what you can do today" says it all. Face those problems head on.

In Psalm 34:19, it states, "A righteous man may have many troubles but the Lord delivers him from them all." For instance, loneliness is a problem many people cannot overcome. One sure way to never feel alone is to start your walk of faith by accepting Jesus Christ as your Savior. Verbally confess your sins and welcome Jesus Christ into your life. Going through the process of accepting Jesus Christ as your Savior is like being reborn and acknowledging you are now a child of God.

In John 14:6 he reports, Jesus answered, "I am the way and the truth and the life. No one comes to the Father except through me." Coming from a Catholic background, I decided to change my religious path at the age of fifty because the Catholic Church was not giving me the knowledge I was seeking about God. One Sunday my family was invited to Greenwell Springs Baptist Church. This Sunday experience was overwhelming because I was in surroundings that I was not accustomed to seeing in a church. Normally I expect the church to be filled with religious statues and encased stained glass murals of Saints looking down at the churchgoers as they quietly take a seat in the nearest pew daring not to call attention to their presence; the atmosphere in this Baptist church was completely opposite. As I entered this massive church with high ceilings held in place with light-colored walls and no religious statutes in sight, numerous people came up to me asking if I was a visitor, if I belong to a bible study group, if I needed anything from them or the church, and everyone appeared to have a "thank you for joining us" attitude. Not ready for the "we are one big happy family" church, I quickly sat down hoping to become invisible in the pew until the service started. As soon as the clock struck 10:30 a.m., the large choir stood up in the designated choir section and joyfully started singing hymns with great enthusiasm.

Loud clapping by the audience followed the tempo of the first hymn. Now understand that in a Catholic church we do not clap, so this experience took me by total surprise. Over to the right of church, I witnessed several people raising their arms up toward the ceiling as if they were asking God to touch them at that moment. Even though I did not know the hymns, I quickly found myself humming the tune, clapping with the choir, and enjoying the energy this large congregation was projecting. One hymn down, and three to go. This church service is going to be fun I thought to myself. When the next song started, the melody sounded like angels singing as the choir harmonized with the lead singer. As I witnessed the conviction in the choir director's face revealing his love for Jesus, I found myself longing for that same strong relationship he openly had with Jesus Christ.

While I had always thought of myself as a religious person, never had I publically expressed my faith as these fellow churchgoers proudly expressed their faith both physically and emotionally that day. As the third hymn started, I felt the spirit of God pass through me, to the point that my skin started tingling, and tears started streaming down my face for no known reason. I gladly held my head up, not embarrassed at all by my sudden bursts of emotions. I knew that day this church was offering me an experience I wanted to continue to explore and invest in for my spiritual growth.

After the choir completed their spiritual jubilation, the church's pastor entered the stage to speak to his congregation. He walked with confidence, knowing the words he was about to share were the Words of God. He carried himself as a proud warrior of God. In his hands, he carried only his Bible; no notes or prepared speech. His lecture was straight from the scripture, straight from his heart, and his message to the congregation was ever so clear. I found myself hanging on to his every word. This church and this pastor taught me how faith is meant to be shared with others. He spent nearly an hour discussing only two passages in the Bible. As he described in detail the purpose of those particular scriptures and how important each and every word meant, I soon realized that the time I had spent reading of the Bible beforehand did not compare to his vast understanding of the Bible. At that moment, I wanted to understand the Bible more. Those powerful words he so eloquently conveyed that morning stirred up my soul. Needless to say, I was totally captivated by the entire worship experience that day.

Belonging to a church is so important and is a great way to conquer loneliness. Members of a church look out for one another. Using the term *brother and sister* becomes real to you because these members consider themselves your extended family. You may already belong to a church; do you get excited about going to church every Sunday, or do you look for excuses why you should not attend? If you said yes to the latter, then you are not in the right church. Look for a church that quenches your loneliness, satisfies your hunger for God's touch, and motivates you to continually strengthen your faith by studying the Bible and praying to God daily.

As you finish this chapter, stop and thank God for giving you this time to reflect on your blessings, and to praise Him for the future blessings He has in store for you. Stand strong in faith. He is in control of your life. He never wavers and never leaves your side. Praise Him for His glory and let Him know you are ready to turn your problems over to Him, knowing through His guidance these problems will soon go away.

Remember, when things get crazy or out of control, say "God, thank you for being in control." He is always there waiting for you to let Him lead you to the path of righteousness and peace.

3

Weeds with Strong Roots

Have you ever experienced johnsongrass growing in your garden? No matter how much you pull it or poison it, the grass comes back with a vengeance, growing taller than any other flower in your garden as if to say, "You can't get rid of me that easy." Johnsongrass has a strong root system, and the only way to truly kill it is to dig down into the soil and destroy its roots.

Many problems we face in our lives are like the roots of johnsongrass. While the problem initially seems to have an easy fix, the solution to the problem is more complicated than it appears. Like johnsongrass, you need to find the root of the problem in order to solve the multitude of issues you may be dealing with today.

One good example of the type of problem I am referring to is being overweight. Struggling with being overweight my entire life, I have tried all of the newest fad diets available over-the-counter and also those under the supervision of a physician. And with every diet, I succeed in the short term to lose the weight and feel great; but as time lingers, my bad eating habits return, making my weight tip the scales more than it did before I got on the diet of the week.

At fifty-three years of age, I finally realized fad diets do not work. Through prayer, I have learned to realize this shell of a body was given to me by God. As I become overweight from eating the chocolates, chips, or ice cream in excess, the proof of my indulgence is in the pounds that are added to the frame of my body. The diets are temporary solutions to a problem that is far deeper than the ability to eat less. To truly have the weight we desire, we must change our eating habits. Our body is the only one God will give us. The more fattening things we eat, the more harm we are doing to our future health. I have learned a simple trick: eat the food God made and not the fast food made by man. You will lose weight. But I promise you this, even with all the knowledge I have about nutrition and consumption amounts, I struggle daily with my food choices. It is always easier to eat foods processed in fast food chains than good foods cooked at home and made with the right ingredients. I add to my daily prayer for God to help me make the right food choices and to give me the strength to turn away from the temptation of foods that could be harmful to my health.

When you start your spiritual path with Jesus Christ, be careful you do not have the same turnout as I did with the numerous fad diets. You get excited about church, go about a month or so, and then start thinking of reasons why you cannot go to church as life gets in your way.

This lack of committed discipline is the start to a road of failure. Like the no-fail diet, to be successful in faith, you need to change your habits, prioritizing God above all things in your life. At this point, you may be saying, "Oh, is religion going to take a lot of work on my part? Can't I just say I believe in Jesus Christ, and I am done and ready to receive my heavenly rewards?" It is my opinion that when you make your verbal declaration of Jesus Christ being your Savior, you are just beginning your journey in faith.

You could just stop there and not look for what lies ahead in your future of faith. Like a baby who has just learned to walk, you should want to take the necessary steps to find ways to nurture your soul, embrace the Bible as the tool needed to make you the best "faith gardener" you can be. The more you learn about our gracious Jesus Christ and His power, the more you find complete peace in knowing His love will always be with you. "For I am the Lord, your God, who takes hold of your right hand and says to you, do not fear, I will help you" (Isaiah 41:13).

Our seeds of faith, hope, and unconditional love of our Jesus Christ have strong roots. With a strong faith, we can overcome problems and be ministers to others who do not have strong roots of faith. When Jesus Christ walked the earth, He carefully selected twelve men who would be the founders of our Christian faith. Those disciples, Peter, Andrew, James, John, Philip, Bartholomew, Thomas, Matthew, James, Lebbaeus, Simon, and Judas, all came from different work backgrounds but believed as one that Jesus Christ was the Son of God.

Jesus called these men to preach about His birth, death, and resurrection throughout the world. While they followed the wishes of Jesus Christ and ministered across the continents, through the pages of history, each disciple suffered a horrible death. The evil weeds of the world worked against their efforts to minister the news of Jesus Christ throughout the world. However, the seeds of their faith produced strong roots of hope we Christians still follow today.

Let us take a moment and think of our relationship with Jesus Christ. Have you grown up in a faith-based home where parents taught you the importance of prayer and the value of your relationship with Jesus? If so, you have been blessed with a strong religious root system. What if you did not grow up in that type of religious family? Are you doomed? Of course not! It is never too late to start your walk with Jesus. Do not look back giving the excuse of no religious upbringing as a reason for the lack of faith but look forward starting today knowing Jesus has been patiently waiting for you to come to Him. Just like a seed planted in fertile soil, you can start your walk of faith today and watch how fast your spiritual self will grow with the nourishment of prayer. In Matthew 7:7, Jesus said, "Ask and it will be given, seek and you shall find, knock and the door will be opened to you."

Take time today and thank our Lord God for all blessings that are already available to you and those blessing that have not come your way yet. Ask for the ability to feel His presence when the world seems to have its hands around your throat like a tight turtleneck sweater. Surrender yourself to His Will so as you grow in faith, you will sow seeds of hope to others.

4

Weeds That Poison

Have you ever touched poison ivy, and afterward found yourself covered in tiny bumps that itch to the point of madness? Poison ivy can attach itself to a tree or conveniently hide itself in a bush so we are not even aware we have come in contact with the poisonous weed. There are some people who are so allergic to the plant, they breakout if they even come near it, much less touch the weed.

Like poison ivy that blemishes the skin, lack of trust in someone we love poisons a relationship the same way. Everyone wants to believe the people in their lives have always been truthful with them. We hang on to their every word as truth. Once we discover this person has lied about something, the poison of the lie starts to penetrate our heart.

The first lie may be about spending money, the second lie may be about being faithful in the relationship, and soon the list of lies grows. The point of this discussion is the first lie started the problem. We soon doubt everything that person has said and done. Like the reoccurring allergic reaction to the poison ivy, we never get over the lack of trust we lost in those who deceive us. This lack of trust can lead us to doubt all the rest of the people who come in our lives now and in the future. What a shame not to be able to trust now because of the fault of others in our past.

One truth we know is the Word of God. He does not lead us astray but provides us with daily guidance. He is always there to catch us when we fail. As His child, we focus on His Word, knowing He will always be there for us as our Father and will never allow evil to take root in our heart. While He remains constant in His trust with our souls, we are the ones who drift away from Him and become the untrustworthy ones in this powerful and spiritual relationship. How many times do we seek His guidance when we are in a crisis though we sometimes fall short rarely singing His praises when all is wonderful in our lives?

Just like poison ivy, words from others can touch our souls and foster ill-emotions. For instance, I can be going along and having a great day, and someone calls me with negative comments about anything and everything. I let them steal my joy by allowing the poison of their attitude to change my emotions and take away the glow of happiness I had before. My first reaction is to answer back to them with the same negative attitude securing my ability to be a fierce warrior, but then I stop short remembering I cannot control this person's attitude but I can surely control my own. I then try to imagine the stress this person must be under and alter my voice to project compassion for them instead. While this approach does not always work, at the end of each day, I evaluate my actions with others and ask for forgiveness when my actions fall short in God's eyes.

We cannot change a person's attitude. Too many times people enjoy the misery they dwell in. Like the poison ivy that is found in the garden we learn to stay away from so we do not have an allergic reaction, so must we learn to stay away from those who make us feel less than the wonderful person God has created us to be. Pray for those who do not have their eyes on God because they do not know the peace the soul experiences when the soul has a close relationship with Him. If we can share our experiences with those who do not know God, then God will bless us for helping bring His children back home to Him.

Have you been baptized? Even though Jesus Christ knew He was the Son of God, He felt compelled to be baptized by John the Baptist. In Matthew 3:16, Matthew describes the baptism of Jesus as follows:, "And Jesus when He was baptized, went up straightway out of the water; and lo, the heavens were opened unto to Him and He saw the spirit of God descending like a dove and lighting upon Him."

As a Catholic child, I was baptized at six weeks old. In the Catholic faith, we believe the religious ceremony is a means to wash away the original sin of Adam and Eve. It is also a commitment made by the parents to God to raise their child in a Catholic home. When I joined Greenwell

Springs Baptist Church at the age of fifty, I discovered the meaning of baptism meant something totally different. When a person decides to be baptized later in life, it is his or her public declaration that he or she has accepted Jesus Christ as his or her Savior.

At the age of fifty-three, I decided I wanted to be baptized at Greenwell Springs Baptist Church. As Jesus himself saw the significance of baptism as a symbol of being reborn with the Spirit, I too wanted my soul to be reborn and be filled with the Holy Spirit. Funny fact about being baptized, for me, was the actual dunking of my head under the water. I have a terrible fear of water. Every time I go under water, I stop breathing due to the anxiety of the fear of drowning. Needless to say, the day I was to be baptized, I was the oldest of the eight who were in line to be baptized. As I looked at the seven-year-old standing in front me getting ready to be dunked by our preacher, I giggled at how she had no fear of the water but was more concerned at the audience waiting for her appointment with our preacher. Just the opposite, I could have cared less about the audience watching me because I was more worried about the gurgling and gasping sounds I would make once he held my head under. But much to my amazement, as I entered the water, I felt no fear at all. As I sat down on the bench preparing for the preacher to lower my head backward, all I could think of was how excited I was to be given the special opportunity to experience this special process. As the preacher asked if

I was ready to accept Jesus as my Lord and Savior, I loudly shouted yes and found myself actually pushing backward so I could go underneath the water to experience my rebirth. The entire experience was so wonderful, and to add to the excitement, my daughter decided to be baptized with me that day as well. As we left the baptismal with our change of dry clothes on, we were both met with our family in the church to celebrate our glorious event. Three days after we were baptized, I woke up and decided it was time for me to write down my experiences I had with God over the years. In eight days, I wrote *Earning My Wings*. My story was one I wanted my children and grandchildren to hear and remember. One month later, I had a publisher ready to take on my new project and share my spiritual experiences with the world. While I do not think of myself as an author or minister, I do think I have experiences to share about the power of God and love every opportunity I have to spread God's message of hope to my brothers and sisters.

If we have struggles keeping us from living a full life, struggles keeping us depressed and prohibiting us from seeing the beauty of this world, then perhaps we need to go through the process of being reborn. Start over. Give the soul a new vision of future life and wash the old life away. By declaring our sins, acknowledging our actions have fallen short of God's ways and accepting Jesus as our Savior, we can start afresh and live the remainder of our lives in peace.

"For I know the plans I have for you, declares the Lord, plans to prosper you and not to harm you, plans to give you hope and a future" (Jeremiah 29:11). As we wash away the old soul and come out of the baptismal water with a fresh new soul, immediately start thanking God for the blessings, which have been promised by Him to come our way. Believe He will reward us for our leaps of faith. As God is our Father, He desires for all His children to shine in His light.

As we start this walk of faith, wake up daily, thanking God for the blessing He is sending our way. We thank Him for standing by us while we deal with the weeds that poison our souls. Relax. God knows our past, our present, and our future. We do not need to tell Him our problems. Moses stated "The eternal God is your refuge and underneath are the everlasting arms. He will draw out your enemy before you, saying 'Destroy him'" (Deuteronomy 33:27). Take time now to praise His name and declare He is King of Kings, Lords of Lords, and He will forever dwell in your heart. The key to a strong spiritual relationship with God is to trust Him no matter what happens in our lives.

God holds us in the palm of His hands, and we are protected from the wrongs of the world. Knowing this world is not our final resting place but only a place for us to grow in faith before we join our Father in heaven. It makes all of the stuff we face in life a little less important, don't you think?

5

Perennial versus Annual

Annual and perennial plants are planted in the spring, grow through summer, and die once the first frost touches the winter ground. However, unlike the annual plant, perennials have the ability to reproduce themselves from their seeds dropped in the surrounding soil or from a strong root system buried beneath the ground. Many times these plants will multiply in such numbers the gardener will be able to share the new additional plants with family and friends. Perennials dominate my garden with continuous blooms throughout the year. It is always fun to go into the garden to see what new flowers come up from the season before. The plants have multiplied so much I have no more room for adding new plants. Letting nature do its own landscaping exceeds anything I could do with my own two hands.

Consider our faith in God. Do we profess to believe in God, live a Christian life, and think that is all that is needed to enter the gates of heaven? Like the annual plant that blooms in spring, our testimony sounds great, and we may be admired by others for the way we wear faith on our sleeve. But in the case of the annual flower, as winter comes, the plant is destroyed and soon forgotten by all. Now think about this for a moment. Does our faith collapse when problems occur, leaving us to question why God has allowed those problems to destroy our peace. Remember, my brothers and sisters, God only gives us what we can handle.

In 1 Corinthians 10:13, Paul states, "There hath no temptation taken you but such as is common to man: but God is faithful, who will not suffer you to be tempted above that ye are able; but will with the temptation also make a way to escape, that ye may be able to bear it." When we question His love for us, our faith is lacking. The roots of our faith should be so strong there is nothing thrown at us that can take our focus off God and His grace. Like the perennial plant that dies down from the frost but reappears in the spring, God plants the seeds of hope in people and gives us endless opportunity to overcome the crisis we are struggling within our lives.

Have you ever thought perhaps maybe the problem placed in your lap is a test of your faith? As I walk in my faith, I am challenged, sometimes hourly, with problems. It appears the more I focus on the Lord above, the problems come down in buckets. I always smile and say quietly, "Satan, is that the best you've got?" because I know God will help me through each crisis. I confess I wish my walk of faith would give me a free pass on problems every once in a while, but it does not. Have you ever looked up and said out loud, "Why Lord is this happening to me? I am one of the good guys!" Well, let me be the first to say, "Been there and done that." But you know, it is that moment of silence after you shout your frustration that chills the air around you. As you search for the answers, stop and take time to thank God for the problems you *do not* have to face today.

While you may be fully overwhelmed by your circumstances, look around you and not very far there are people in your life suffering from countless misery. Talk to your neighbor and see how he is doing. He may be going through a life-threatening illness with no hope of recovery. Talk to a coworker who has seemed distant to everyone at the office the past few weeks. She may have just been told by her husband he wanted a divorce, and she had no clue they were having marriage troubles. Now focus back on your problem. It may be huge to you, but remember God does not give you more than you can handle. Put everything in prospective. Live one day at a time and always know you are not alone. You cannot change what happened yesterday and you have no control on tomorrow. Live the best you can today under God's wing.

David stated "A righteous man may have many troubles but the Lord delivers him from them all" (Psalm 34:19). Answer this question. Do you believe in the Word of our Lord? Of course you do, or you would have put this book down three chapters earlier. The point is you have His Word. He will deliver us from the troubles of the world. So remember the next time you are in that 3:00 a.m. silent time, frantically wondering what to do about your problem, get down on your knees and pray, truly pray for God to deliver you from these troubles. He loves you and already knows your troubles. He needs you to surrender your heart to Him, and trust He will see you through the troubles. I spend a lot of time on my knees praying because I know it is there at that moment God and I are having our one-on-one time that no one else can take away from us.

After a violent storm passes, a rainbow appears; the rain cleanses the land and allows nature to grow. Same with you, my brother and sister—after the storm of your troubles pass, believe something good will come from it because you allowed God to maintain control of your situation. Be patient for God to work His wonders. You may not receive the relief as fast as you want, but remember God knows the master plan and the rest of your story. He will help you through the problems in His time and not in yours. There is a reason for everything in our lives, and it is not for us to question His judgment when dealing with struggles.

Like the thorns on a rose, everything has a purpose or happens for a reason. God allows the weeds to exist in our lives for a purpose. Our mission in life is to find out what the purpose is and make the best of it.

6

Spending Time in Your Garden

Imagine walking in your own garden now. Do you look for weeds, or do you admire the flowers first? This is a trick question. Many people get stuck on their problems so much that when they are around others, all they want to discuss is how everyone and everything is doing them wrong. Me, me, me is all you hear from them. Sometimes when you are around those who have mastered this selfish skill, you find yourself wanting to run the opposite direction, to get away from them because you know you do not have forty-five minutes or more to hear about *them*. These are people who look at the weeds and do not take the time to see the flowers of blessings in their lives.

They fail to see the wonderful people God has put in their path, as well as the opportunities they have been given in their life. They may have a great job, but they think they do not make enough money. They have a wonderful house with an affordable payment, but they believe they need a bigger house to impress their friends. Again, they are looking for the weeds and are not seeing the beautiful blessings they have been given by God.

To find peace in our lives, I believe we must dwell on the good we have; we must look at the flowers in our garden of life. Like any garden, it will have weeds. Like any life, we will have problems. But through our faith in God, the good in our life will always outweigh the bad. If you are experiencing overwhelming problems and cannot see any good in your life, stop and pray to God, our Father. God will show you what your brain denies your soul to see.

In John 15:5–6, Jesus said, "I am the vine, you are the branches. Whoever abides in me and I in him, he is that bears much fruit, for apart from me, you can do nothing. If anyone does not abide in me he is thrown away like a branch and withers; and the branches are gathered, thrown into the fire and burned." Having Jesus as our Savior should be the focal point in our spiritual garden. With His love, our garden of life will be filled with peace. Like the flowers blooming in the garden, providing pollen for the bees, Jesus freely gives us His love to enjoy forever.

In the Bible, there are numerous stories of how the evil actions of people prohibit others from enjoying their garden of life. For instance, we all know the story where Cain, the son of Adam and Eve, killed his brother Abel. But as you follow the genealogy of his family forward, he did not flourish in life as Seth his younger brother. Ironically, eight generations from Seth, Noah was born and was instructed by God to build the ark that would save Noah and his family from the great flood, while the remainder of the people, including all of Cain's descendants, perished in the great flood.

In Matthew 13:3–23, Jesus spoke,

> Behold a sower went forth to sow; and when he sowed, some seeds fell by the way side, and the fowls came and devoured them up; Some fell upon stony places, where they had not much earth; and forthwith they sprung up, because they had no deepness of earth; And when the sun was up they were scorched; and because they had no root, they withered away; And some fell among thorns; and the thorns sprung up and choked them; But other fell into good ground, and brought forth fruit, some an hundredfold, some sixtyfold, some thirtyfold; Who hath ears to hear, let him hear.

In comparison to the *seeds that fall by the way side*, how many times do we read scripture, not relate to its meaning, and quickly disregard the content because the passage did not "scream out" to us in simple terms? As you read the Bible, do you still feel lost from the passages? Do you read and push back saying, "What does this mean?" So, as a result of your frustration, you close the Bible, shake your head, and walk away from any opportunity to learn the word of God.

Too many times in our lives, if things require significant work on our part, we quickly make excuses for not doing the work necessary to complete the task. When we give up or ignore reading the Bible faithfully, we fall short on our duty to study the Word of God and take the time to dig out its meaning, as my pastor once told me.

An example of *seeds that fall on stony places* is the test of our faith during troubled times. For example, as trouble comes our way, we sometimes lose faith and turn toward despair and destruction instead of hope. We must build a strong base of faith, knowing whatever obstacles we will have to endure, God is there for us and will see us through this violent storm. Our roots of faith will keep us steady through rough times.

Say during these times, "All is well because God is still on the throne." When something hits you harder than before, say it a little louder with conviction. Personally, when I am hit with challenges, I say that phrase to myself but add a little caveat, "Poor, poor Satan, is that the best you have got?" I laugh at his powerless ways to diminish my faith. Now I will be the first to say Satan will tempt even the strongest Christians. Recognize you are in control of your love for God. Surrender your heart in the name of Jesus Christ, and appreciate He is in control of your situation. You no longer are like the seed growing in the stony place, but more like the seed growing in fertile soil.

Have you ever thought free will is analogous to *seeds that fall in the thorns*? Free will gives us the ability to have whatever we desire in life. If we are ambitious, we can have a fabulous career, make tons of money, and have all the toys our hearts desire. But like the seeds that fall in the thorns, the love of money can choke out our love for God. We must always put God first in our lives. Is He first in your life?

Take this simple test. In the morning when you first wake, eyes open looking at the time on the clock, what comes to your mind? Do you instantly smile and thank God for the blessings He will be sending your way? Do you thank Him for giving you one more day to share with your loved ones? Or do you immediately start thinking of the laundry list of things you need to do today? At those early hours when all is quiet, dedicate that special time each morning to pray.

Always remember that you are promised today only. No one is guaranteed tomorrow. As you begin to appreciate every moment of your day and share the gratitude with God, He will smile upon your life.

It is amazing how precious those moments with God can be. And at the end of the day when work is over, kids are asleep, and you are done with the day's routine, do you stop and thank God for another day, for helping you through the troubles, and for putting certain people in your path who made your life a little better that day? You must realize He was with you all during the day. In the busiest part of the day, how many times did you think of Him? I always finish every night with a prayer. I believe we cannot let the thorns of our lives choke out the precious time we spend with God.

A seed that falls on good fertile ground and brings forth fruit in abundance is analogous to someone who has strong faith in the Lord, practices his faith daily, and looks for opportunities to share the Word of the Lord with others. How simple can it be? As you surrender your life to Christ, you are reborn with the Holy Spirit nestled around your soul like a seed planted in fertile soil. As the seed in the fertile soil needs water, you must continue your study in faith, seek others who will guide you spiritually, and nurture others who have lost their spiritual way.

We are not meant to stand in our faith alone. Faith in God is meant to be shared with others. As our seed of hope grows strong in this fertile soil of the Holy Spirit, our roots of faith will grow long and wide, anchoring our soul in God's Kingdom. As the plant that struggles in drought, we too will have challenges in our faith. But we must take these challenges as an opportunity to strengthen our faith.

Take your Bible, open it up to whatever page your eyes first see, and start reading the Word. Read like you have never read before. Ask God to speak to you through the passages of the Bible, and I promise you will find comfort. If you try and find no comfort, then you are standing in your own way. God is there beside you, but your heart is not in it. Please go back to the Bible and try again. I promise you will find the answers you seek in the Bible because His Word was written for all of us to read.

The Seasons of Life

A garden is ever evolving. In spring, you prepare the flower beds, plant seeds or young plants in preparation for a harvest later in the year. As we breathe our first breathe, we are introduced to people who will influence our character. Consider God as the number one Gardener. He gives us life and plants us in the place where we will grow. Like a garden overgrown with weeds, our lives are faced with many problems. But with His love and His promise, we will flourish in the garden of life, as we continue to keep our eyes and heart focused only on Him.

Summer is the time when the garden has its fullest potential to grow. As in life, we grow up to be adults, leave home, and start our lives. Those who continue to focus on God's love, never losing sight of His guidance, will continue to grow spiritually. Like seeds on a plant, we give birth to our children who will carry on our name. It is our responsibility to be the best role models we can be in order to teach to them about God and give them the spiritual nourishment they need to understand God and His grace.

As we nurture our children in Jesus' teachings, they too will never feel alone. They will ensure their place in heaven and will be able to educate and nurture their children in faith. If you do not want to share the love of Jesus with your children, then who do you think will teach them? Do you not love them enough that you want to make sure their souls have a place in heaven? How sad if you get to heaven and realize they are not there. In Hebrews 12:15, Paul states, "A bitter root that grows up to cause trouble and defile many."

Fall is the time of harvest. In the latter part of our life, our children are grown, moved away, and it is the time to retire from our career. As we look back on our harvest of life, we proudly look back at our works, marvel at our children and our grandchildren, and take comfort that all of life's efforts produced a wonderful life.

I believe fall is also a time for us to reflect on the newness that is awaken when everything else seems to be getting ready for a winter's nap. For instance, have you ever witnessed a patch of spider lilies blooming in the most unexpected places? This delicate dark-red flower, with curvy petals and long stems that support the bloom, appear out of nowhere, making the other dull plants and dying grass fade into the background of its presence. As I approach the fall in my life, I view these flowers as reminders that there is still bloom left in my days. As with the spider lilies, the blooms of my life will come more random than in the spring of my life. But what joy it is now to look forward to the surprise of the possibilities that lie ahead of me before my winter comes. With continued faith in the promise of Jesus' return, we all can count the spider lilies in our lives as bonus blessings.

Winter is the time for sleep. A time when most trees go dormant, most flowers die, and many animals hibernate. As in life, death is our winter. We go to sleep with the promise from God that we will rise again and be with Him in heaven.

After Jesus died on the cross, he rose again on the third day. He later walked the earth for forty days to let everyone know he was real and is still alive in all of us today. Throughout the Christian biblical teachings, we know Jesus died on the cross to wash away our sins. The sins of man are endless: from Adam to Eve's disobedience to God, to Cain killing his brother Abel, to the sins we commit today such as greed, lust, and lack of commitment to God. Jesus had to suffer a horrible death from the beatings, the piercing of his hands and feet, to the hanging from the cross as a sacrifice for our sins so we could be forgiven by God and enter into the gates of heaven as children of God.

Paul writes "Let us fix our eyes on Jesus, the author and finisher of our faith who for the joy that was set before Him endured the cross, despairing the shame and is set down at the right hand of the throne of God" (Hebrew 12:2). I believe Jesus is a Savior hero for everyone. Before Jesus' birth, throughout the Old Testament, God shows numerous accounts where He favored the Israelites. "Moses told his people, 'For those art holy people unto the Lord thy God. The Lord thy God hath chosen thee to be a special people unto Himself, above all people that are upon the face of the earth'" (Deut. 7:6). For example, Moses parted the Red Sea so God's chosen people could escape from the Egyptians. God fed them when they were hungry and provided water for them when they were thirsty.

With Jesus' birth and resurrection, Christianity was born, and this faith is made available to all people and all nations who accept them as their Savior. In John 14:6, when Thomas asks Jesus how they would find their way when Jesus was gone, Jesus answered, "I am the way and the truth and the life. No one comes to the Father except through Me." I believe because Jesus lived and died for us, we as followers of Jesus become God's *chosen children*, which is not the same as God's *chosen people*. We can all agree a parent's love for a child far outweighs the love one has for a friend. As a child of God, we rest in peace, knowing He will always love and protect us.

In conclusion, be a good gardener. Pay attention to the weeds in your life and destroy them as soon as they come up. Look for and appreciate the flowering blessings you have been given. "This is the day the Lord has made; let us rejoice and be glad in it. Our lives are short" (Psalm 118:24).

As certain as winter will come, death will also. Have your garden of life in pristine condition so it will continue to grow long after you are gone, because of the life with God you lived. In heaven you can help the angels send the rain of blessings to the garden of the family you left behind. The love you left with them will continue to grow even though you are no longer there with them.

I end this book with a prayer for you.

I pray you open your spiritual eyes today and see the garden God has laid before you. I pray you plant your seeds of faith in Jesus Christ. And I pray for you, my brothers and sisters, the Holy Spirit continues to fill your soul with the nourishment needed to master the gardening of your faith.

Amen.

Afterword

The garden referred to in this book is a garden located in my yard, not created by me, but by the previous owner. They named this special place the "Mother and daughter love garden." The family built the meandering flowerbeds, laid the brick sidewalk that flows throughout, and placed a picket fence around the entire garden to protect its precious contents. Inside the garden, they built a potting shed which resembles an old cottage made of aged cypress, topped with a tin roof, and crowned with a copper weather vane sailboat. All plants were carefully selected perennials that promise blooms throughout the seasons for years to come.

For the first few years, I hated the garden because of the amount of work it required to be maintained. The endless weeding project brought little joy to me. While others admire and compliment over the multitude of blooms it projects, all I could see was the enormous wrath of weeds it contained within its walls. One week before I had scheduled the garden to be bulldozed down, a friend came by to visit us. He knew the family that had lived in our home previously and proceeded to tell us about their misfortune. In 2013, their only daughter took a sailing trip off the coast of New Zealand. Three days out to sea, the boat, the Nina, with the crew and their only daughter came up missing. The search for her continues to this day.

As I walked through the garden later that day, I realized this garden represented all of the love that mother and daughter shared while they lived here. There was no way I could tear down this garden. So instead, I began changing my attitude about it. I started appreciating the beauty the garden projected and developed a maintenance routine that keeps my "weed anxiety" down to a minimum.

This garden is a symbol of my faith in God's protection over Danielle and a commitment of hope that when she returns, she will come back to this childhood home and will see everyone in her life and this special garden have been waiting for her return.